# GIGANT

4

BY HIROYA OKU

SEVEN SEAS ENTERTAINMENT PRESENTS

# GIGANT™

story and art by HIROYA OKU VOLUME 4

TRANSLATION
Christine Dashiell

ADAPTATION
Jamal Joseph Jr.

LETTERING
Ray Steeves

INTERIOR LAYOUT
Christa Miesner

ORIGINAL COVER DESIGN
Yohei Sometani

COVER DESIGN
Nicky Lim

PROOFREADER
Kurestin Armada

EDITOR
J.P. Sullivan

PREPRESS TECHNICIAN
Rhiannon Rasmussen-Silverstein

MANAGING EDITOR
Julie Davis

ASSOCIATE PUBLISHER
Adam Arnold

PUBLISHER
Jason DeAngelis

GIGANT VOLUME 4
by Hiroya OKU


Seven Seas press and purchase enquiries can be sent to Marketing Manager Lianne Sentar at press@gomanga.com. Information regarding the distribution and purchase of digital editions is available from Digital Manager CK Russell at digital@gomanga.com.



ISBN: 978-1-64505-946-2

Printed in Canada

First Printing: January 2021

10 9 8 7 6 5 4 3 2 1

FOLLOW US ONLINE: *www.sevenseasentertainment.com*

## READING DIRECTIONS

This book reads from ***right to left***, Japanese style. If this is your first time reading manga, you start reading from the top right panel on each page and take it from there. If you get lost, just follow the numbered diagram here. It may seem backwards at first, but you'll get the hang of it! Have fun!!

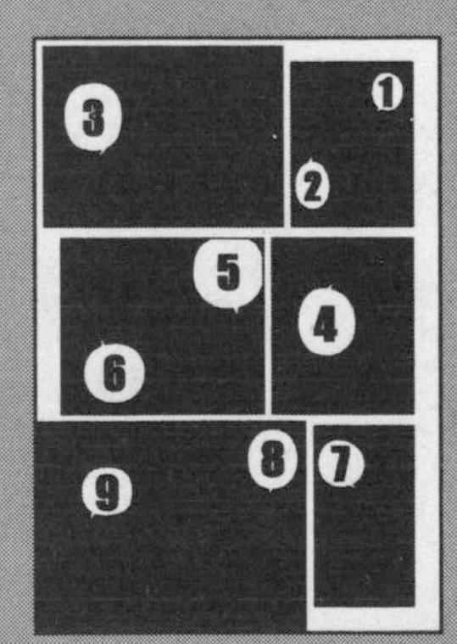

GIGANT™

THE NEXT CHAPTER…

"GIGANT" CHAPTER FOUR : END TO BE CONTINUED _

EEEEEEEEK!
パチ CLAP
パチ CLAP
パチ CLAP
パチ CLAP
パチ CLAP
パチ CLAP
パチ CLAP
ぴょ HOP
ぴょ HOP
P-PAPICO-- PAPICO HAS JUST EMERGED FROM WITHIN THE GIANT!!
SHE TORE HER WAY THROUGH IT!!

メキ
SPLITCH
メキ
SPLATCH
メキ
SPLUTCH

HGRK
HGRK
HGRK
HGRK

TWITCHING. SHAKING. IT ALMOST REMINDS ME OF AN ANIMAL TRYING TO BRUSH OFF AN INSECT!

GO...

GO!!

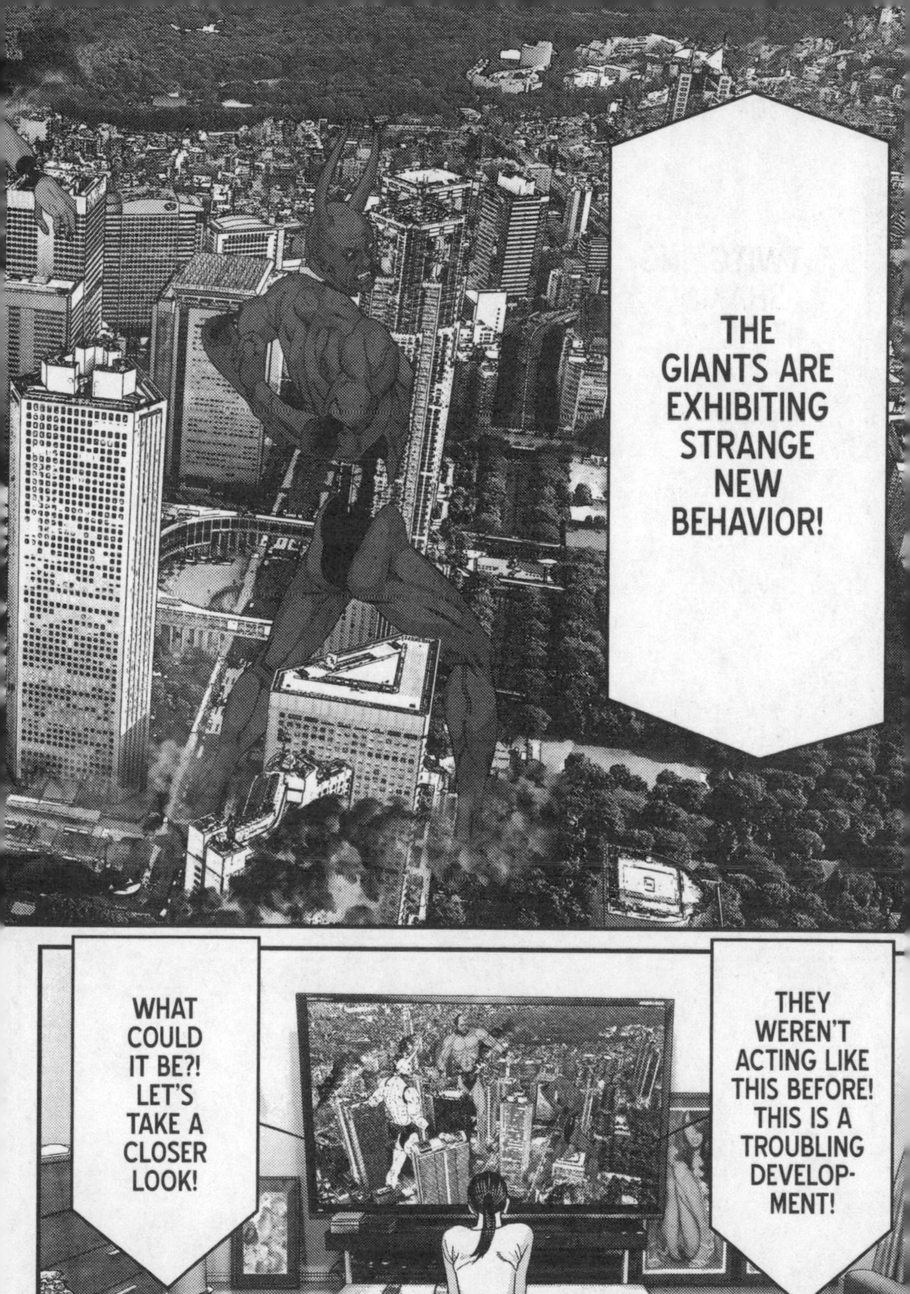
THE GIANTS ARE EXHIBITING STRANGE NEW BEHAVIOR!
THEY WEREN'T ACTING LIKE THIS BEFORE! THIS IS A TROUBLING DEVELOP-MENT!
WHAT COULD IT BE?! LET'S TAKE A CLOSER LOOK!

HUFF!
HUFF!
HUFF!

ゴオオオオオ
SHWOOOOOOO
HUFF!
HUFF!
BOOM
ドン

★Apricot★@mangaero - 50s
They're saying she disappeared... What do they mean?
#shinjuku
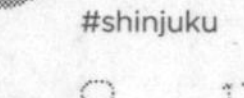

Alice @ Kawazaki @ishikawa_a - 45s
It looked like they'd torn her apart...
#shinjuku
Ice13 @ant_was - 30s
How can the station air this gore-fest?!
#shinjuku

Yoshio @ Suehirocho @yoshio_t2 -
What's going down? Word was PaPiCo got got...

Bean torpedo @mamegyo - 20s
Now what? The SDF couldn't get them, and PaPiCo's dead. Time to go nuclear?

Red Mercury @ Ueno @red_m
Give it up... Tokyo's done for...
#shinjuku

THEY'RE SAYING PAPICO'S DEAD...
THEY SAY SHE GOT RIPPED APART.
NOW WHAT DO WE DO? COME ON... JUST STAY LIKE THIS?

NO...
THIS ISN'T... ENOUGH ...
TO KILL...
CHIHO-SAN...

IT LOOKED AS THOUGH PAPICO COLLAPSED...
I SWEAR... WHAT'S GOING ON HERE? SHE'S DISAPPEARED.

IT SEEMS PAPICO REALLY HAS VANISHED!
THE GIANTS LOOK LIKE THEY'RE SCANNING FOR HER WHEREABOUTS, TOO!
NO...
IT'S JUST LIKE LAST TIME ...

HUFF!
HUFF!
HUFF!

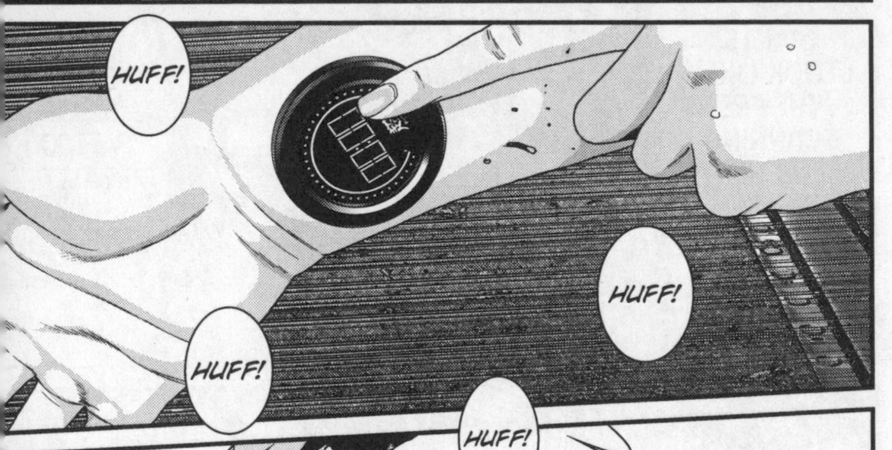
HUFF!
HUFF!
HUFF!

HUFF!
THERE'S NO WAY...
YOU'RE GONNA BEAT ME!!
HUFF!

HAAH!
BOOM
BOOM
BOOM
HUFF!

HUFF!
HUFF!

HUFF!

HUFF!
HUFF!
HUFF!

PAPICO... SHE'S...!

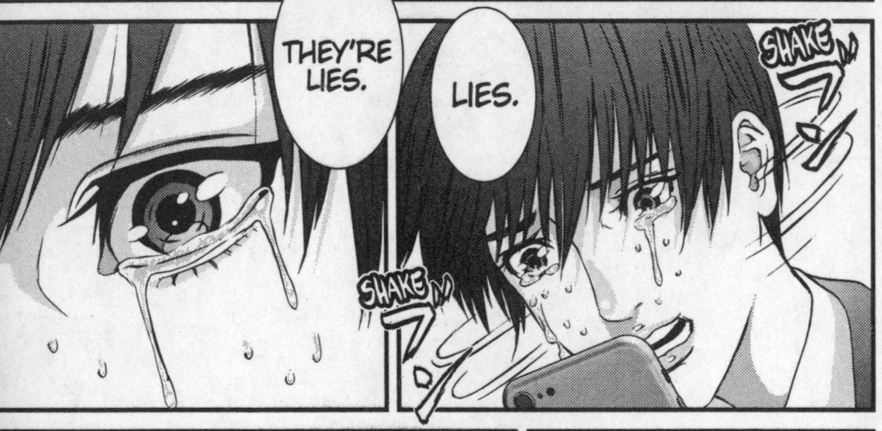

THEY'RE LIES.
LIES.
SHAKE
SHAKE

What do we do...?

#shinjuku

**Misoko Nuts!** @MHnagih

PaPiCo's limbs got torn off and dropped...

#shinjuku

**Hell Sniper** @hellsniper

I wish they'd stop it with all the gore

#papico
#shinjuku

**Key-free** @magicalto

Huh? Am I seeing this right? It looks like she disappeared...

#giants

AAH!
SHE'S DEAD!!
HUH? SHE'S *DEAD?*
THEY SAY HER HEAD WAS RIPPED OFF!

TREMBLE
TREMBLE

AAAAH!
IT'S ALL OVER!!
NO WAY!
HER LIMBS WERE TORN APART?!
I KNEW IT...
A SINGLE PERSON WOULDN'T MEAN SHIT.
THEN PAPICO'S... JUST BEEN **MURDERED.**

CHIHO-SAN.
CHIHO-SAN.
CHIHO-SAN!!
CHIHO-SAN!!
CHIHO-SAN.

GRK
GRK
GRK
GRK
GRK
GRK
GRK
GRK

EPISODE 38: WHEREABOUTS

# EPISODE 38

ETE
enjoy the end
IT LOOKS LIKE E.T.E. HAD SOME MOVEMENT JUST NOW!

A NEW POLL'S BEEN DECIDED UPON BY THE USERS!

HUH?!
WHAT?


**POLL RESULTS**

**"PAPICO IS TORN TO PIECES AND DIES" HAS REACHED FIRST PLACE.**

WHAT THE?! THIS IS... THIS IS TERRIBLE!!

CHIHO-SAA-AN!
CHIHO-SAAA-AAN!

ぐ GRK
ぐ GRK
ぐ GRK

グ GRK
グ GRK
グ GRK

AAAAAAH!
CHIHO-SAAAN!
NOOO!

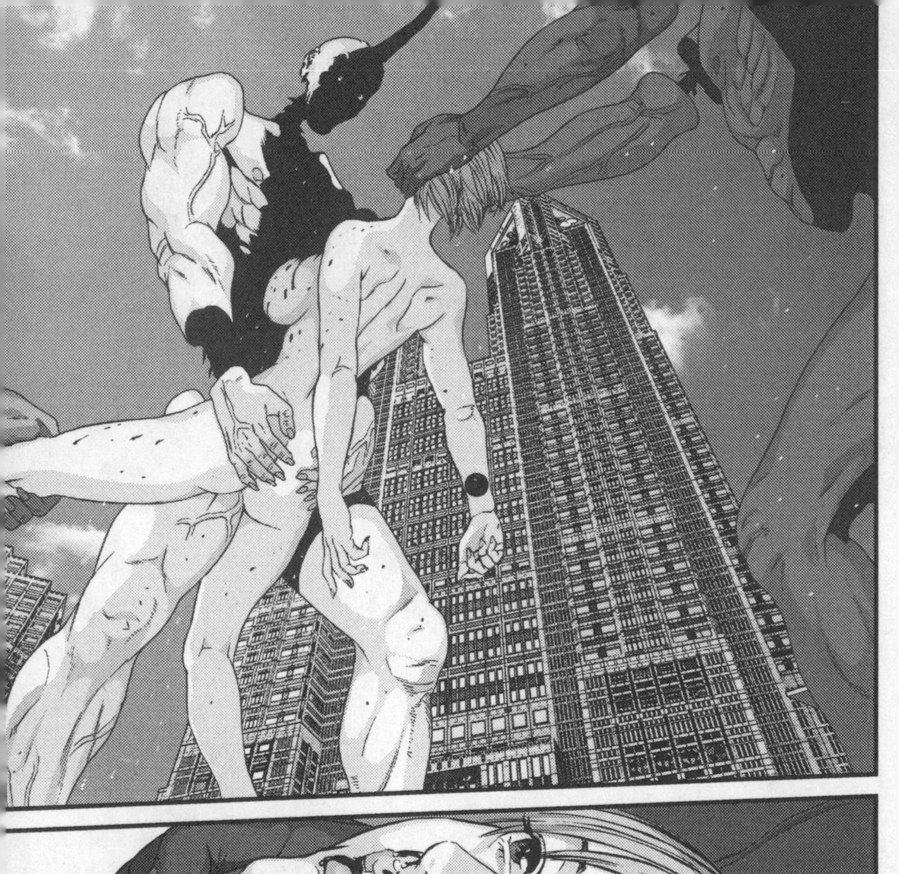

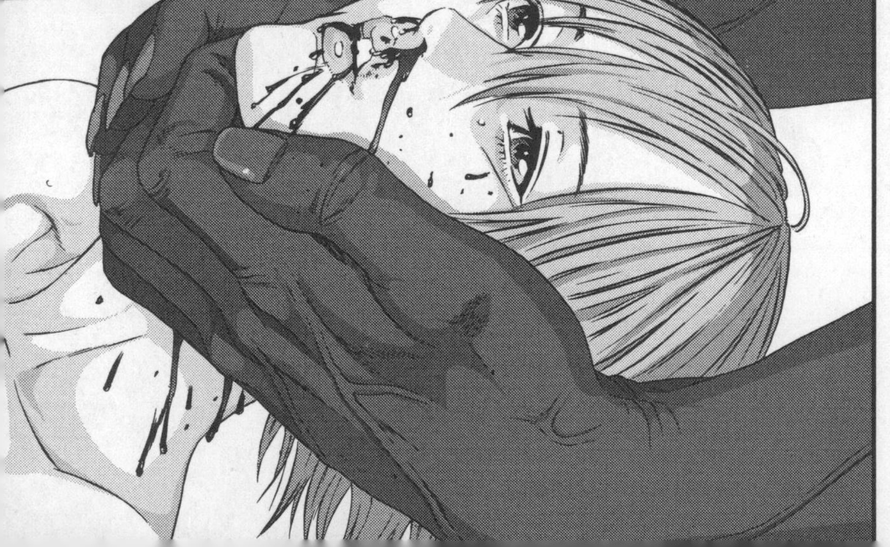

WHERE'S PAPICO? WHAT HAP-PENED TO HER?

UUUUH.
UHHHN...

UUNH.
UUUUH.

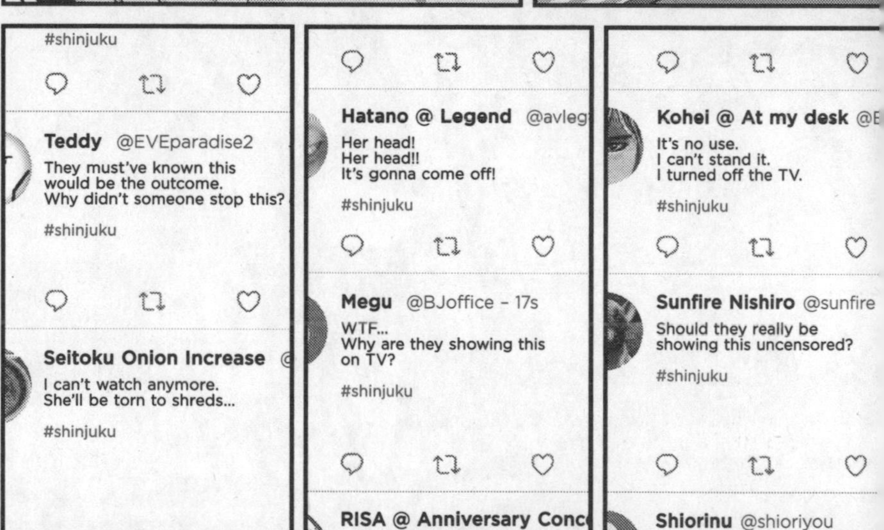
Kohei @ At my desk
It's no use.
I can't stand it.
I turned off the TV.
#shinjuku
Sunfire Nishiro @sunfire
Should they really be
showing this uncensored?
#shinjuku
Shiorinu @shioriyou
Hatano @ Legend @avleg
Her head!
Her head!!
It's gonna come off!
#shinjuku
Megu @BJoffice - 17s
WTF...
Why are they showing this
on TV?
#shinjuku
RISA @ Anniversary Conc
#shinjuku
Teddy @EVEparadise2
They must've known this
would be the outcome.
Why didn't someone stop this?
#shinjuku
Seitoku Onion Increase
I can't watch anymore.
She'll be torn to shreds...
#shinjuku

AAAA-AAH!

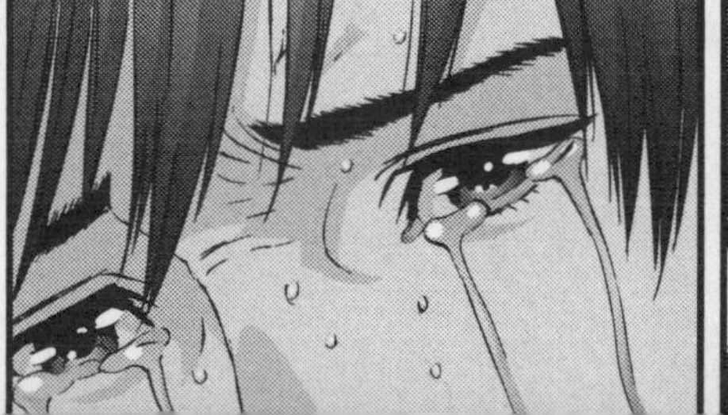

BOOM

BA-
BOOM

NO... NO...
CHIHO-SAN. CHIHO-SAN...

CHIHO-SAN...
CHIHO-SAN...

MR Mind @caterpilla
PaPiCo's in trouble. The nerve, showing this on TV.
#shinjuku

Mix master @MIXMa
AAAAAAAA PAPICOAAAAAAAH!
#shinjuku

NO ...
NO ...

Yellow honey★bee @E
It's no use.
No use, I tell you.
This is bad.
#shinjuku
Yuki @ Here_all_wee
She's gonna die.
Oh man, I can't believe this...
#shinjuku

NO ...
NO ...

Black Cat Felicia @
Pity for them, it's over...
#shinjuku
Makeup Arcee @go
No... If PaPiCo dies now...what are we going to do...?
#shinjuku

OH NO! THEY'RE GANGING UP ON HER!
DAMN! THIS IS BAD!
HUH?
WHAT?
OH NO! THIS IS... NO!
SWITCH TO A PRE-RECORDING!!

BOOM
BA-BOOM

あああ
AAAAH!
パピコ
PAPICO!!
ドーン
BOOM
ドーン
BOOM
BA-
ドーン
BOOM
ゴオオオオ
SHWOOOOO

BOOM
BOOM
55:00
BOOM
BOOM
BOOM
BOOM

WHAM
WHAM
AAAAH!

PAPICO !!
YOU CAN DO IT!!
PAPICO! PAPICO!
PAPICO! PAPICO!

PA-PICO!
PA-PICO!

あああ――っ
AAAAAAH!

WE JUST GOT WORD THAT CHIHO JOHANSSON HAS BEEN GRANTED AMNESTY.
AMNESTY, TO PUT IT SIMPLY, MEANS...
NO... NO, NO.
FORGET THAT!
WHAT ABOUT SHINJUKU?!

I HEARD AMERICA'S BIG THREE NEWS GIANTS ARE BROADCASTING LIVE FROM SHINJUKU.
THE WORLD OVER, ALL EYES ARE ON US.

AND THAT SCARES ME.
WHAT IF THE WORLD WATCHES...
AND PAPICO-SAN FAILS?
I AGREE.
A LIVE BROADCAST... IT'S A GAMBLE.

カラオケ
大明神
ジューン
英会話
新宿本校

めたのーる
小島商

NO...
PLEASE, NO.
NO.
YOU CAN'T.

NO ...
NO.
NO, NO.
SHE CAN'T ...
SHE CAN'T.
IT'S NO USE...
I DON'T WANT THIS...

IT'S PAPICO!
SHE REALLY CAME!

BOOM
BOOM

ドーン
BOOM
ドーン
BOOM

## EPISODE 37: CLOSE UP

WHAAAAA?!
IT'S PAPICO!
SHE'S
HUGE!!
SELF-DEFENSE
FORCE UNIT DESCENDS
EPISODE 37

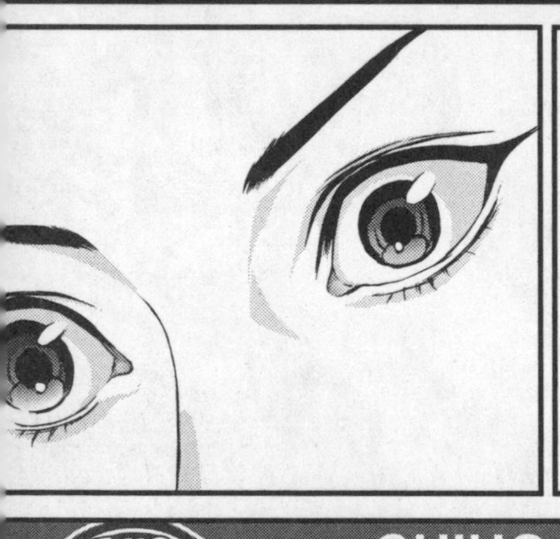

THIS
JUST IN
CHIHO JOHANSSON
GRANTED AMNESTY

オオオオオ
オオ

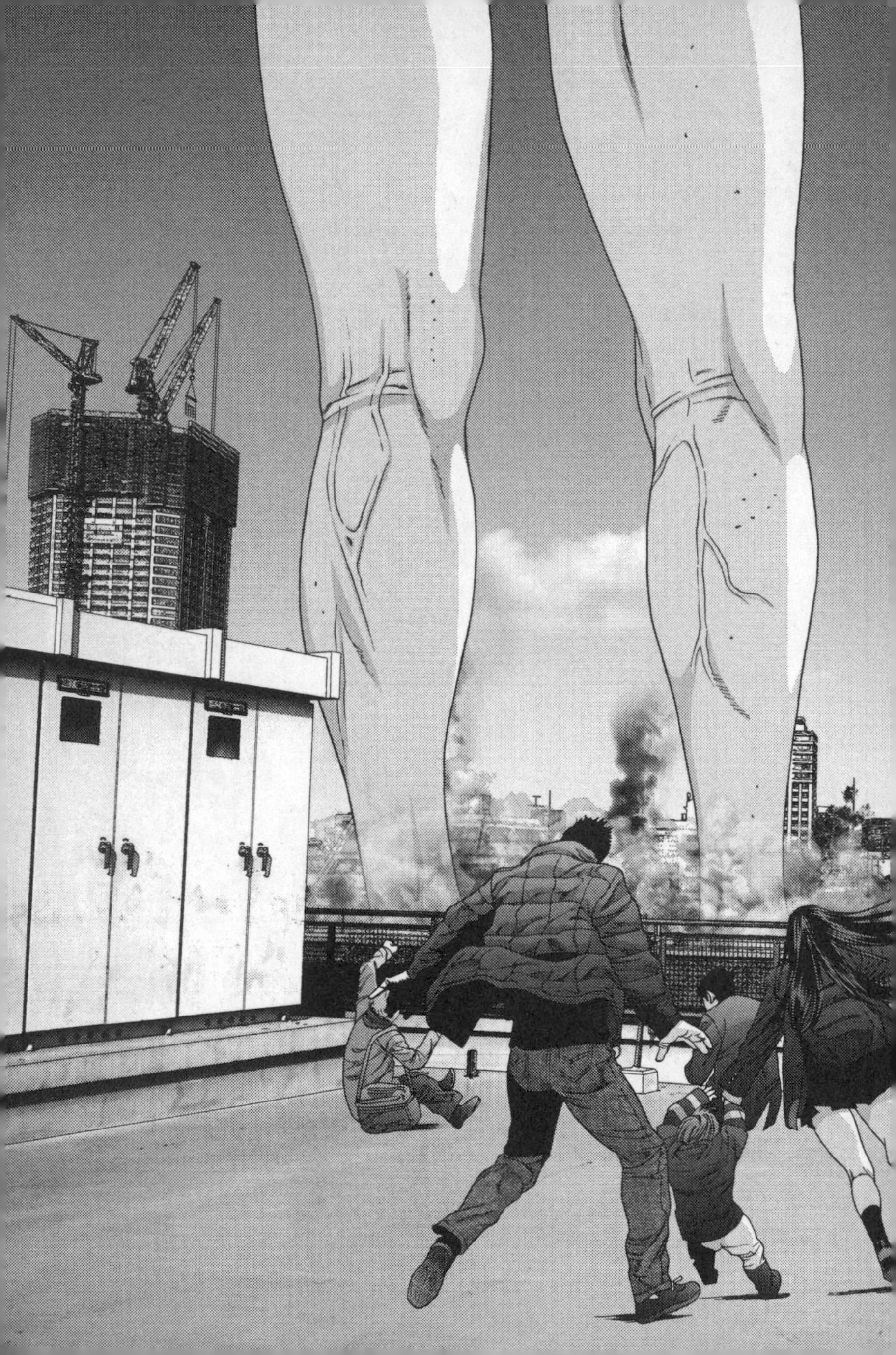

BOOM
BOOM
BOOM
BOOM

BOOM

BOOM
WHOOM
EEEE-YAH!
NOOOO!
BOOM
BOOM
BOOM
MOMMY! I DON'T WANT TO DIE!

AAAAGH!
MOM! MOM!!
I DON'T WANT TO DIE!
I DON'T WANT TO DIE!
THOOM
BOOM
BOOM
BOOM

ドーン BA-BOOM
ガラ CRMBL
ガラ CRMBL
ガラ CRMBL
ドーン BA-BOOM

THOOOOM
BOOM

BA-BA-BOOM
THOOM
B-Breath
Victory
JAR

THOOM
THOOOOM
OUIS LUITTON
OUIS LUITTON
OUIS LUITTON

BOOM
BOOM
BOOM
BOOM

BOOM
BOOM

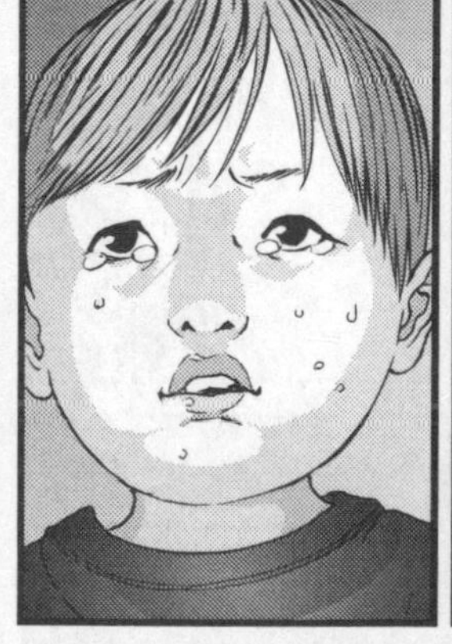

BOOM
BOOM
BOOM
BOOM
BOOM
BOOM

RUMBLE
RUMBLE
RUMBLE
RUMBLE
RUMBLE
RUMBLE
NO! NO!
IT'S NO USE!
RUMBLE
RUMBLE
RUMBLE
RUMBLE
RUMBLE
RUMBLE
RUMBLE
WE'RE DONE FOR!!
RUMBLE
RUMBLE
RUMBLE
MOM
Where in Shinjuku are you?
I'm sorry, mom I think this might b the end for me.
Don't talk that way.
I'm sorry. I'll do what I can. You guys take care...

SHRAK

GWM
GWM
GWM
GWM

BA-DUMP
BA-DUMP
BA-DUMP

BOOMF

HAAH!
HUFF!
HAAH!
NNGH!

BWOOOOOOSH
SCARY. SCARY.
PANT!
PANT!
BWOOOOOOOSH
I'M SO SCARED!
PANT!
PANT!

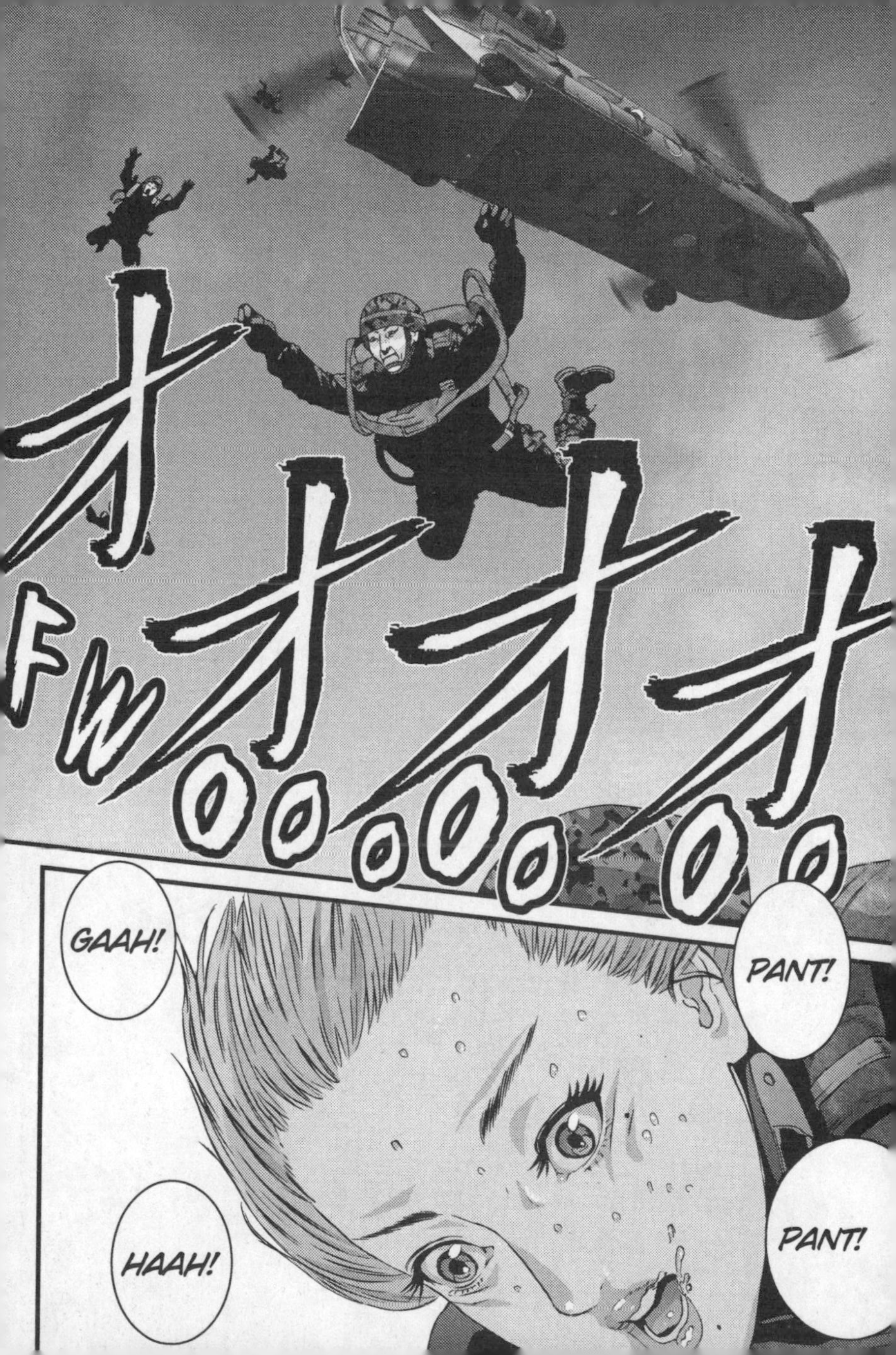
オオオオ
FWOOOOOOO
PANT!
GAAH!
PANT!
HAAH!

EPISODE 36: PAPICO II

EPISODE 36

RRGH...
HUFF!
HUFF!
HUFF!

PANT!
PANT!
PANT!
SHWOOOOOOOO
PANT!
PANT!
BOOM
BOOM
BOOM

THOOM
THOOM
<This way!!>
BOOM
<There's another over there!!>
BOOM
BOOM
BOOM
BOOM

BLAM
BLAM
BLAM
YOU CAN'T DO SHIT TO ME!

OOF!

THUD

BLAM
JUST TRY AND CRUSH ME! JUST TRY!
BLAM
BLAM
BLAM
BLAM
HRAA-AAH!
YAA-AAH!

BOOM
BOOM

ざわ
MURMUR
ざわ
MURMUR
ざわ
MURMUR
BA-
BA-
BOOM
BA-
BOOM

ざわ
MURMUR
ざわ
MURMUR
ざわ
MURMUR
ざわ
MURMUR
ざわ
MURMUR
ざわ
MURMUR

WHOA, WHOA, WHOA, WHOA.
WHAT?
WHAT IS IT?
WHAT'S THE MATTER?
BOOM
BOOM
BOOM
BOOM
BOOM
BOOM
BOOM
BOOM

LOOK AT HER.
THERE'S NO WAY.
AS IF SHE COULD PROTECT US.

はっは
HAR!
HAR
はっ
HAR

I'D LOVE FOR HER TO PROTECT ME, IF Y'KNOW WHAT I MEAN.

YEAH... THOSE TITS!
THEY'RE WICKED HUGE!
WHAT'S HER CUP SIZE?

YOU'RE A DOG.
THAT'S SEXUAL HARASS-MENT.
DON'T ASK QUES-TIONS LIKE THAT.

EYES UP. WE'RE ALMOST THERE...

WRONG. SHE'S THE ONE IT'S ON.
IT'S ONLY *HER* THAT CAN PROTECT US.
I SAW IT ALL.
LIVE ON TV.
はっはっはっはっは
HA HA HA HA HA!

SHE GROWS UP ALL GIANT-LIKE.
BIG ENOUGH TO CRUSH BUILDINGS UNDER-FOOT.
SO WE'RE TAKING HER TO THE SITE.

REAL BIG, YEAH?
YOU WATCH TOO MANY SCI-FI MOVIES, MAN.

YOU CAN'T REALLY MEAN ANY OF THAT.
GET YOUR HEAD ON STRAIGHT.

HEY, IS WHAT THEY SAY TRUE?
THAT YOU CAN GET ALL HUGE?
UH...
YES.

FOR REAL?!
THAT'S A HARD SELL, HONESTLY.

DUDE. HAVEN'T YOU SEEN THE YOUTUBE VIDEO?
THE ONE OF ROP-PONGI.

I HEARD THAT WAS CGI.
THAT'S WHAT PEOPLE ONLINE SAY.

THEN WHY...
ARE WE HERE... TRANS-PORTING HER?

HOW SHOULD I KNOW? WE GOT ORDERS.
THAT'S ALL THAT MATTERS.

ANY-WAY...
S'TIME TO FIX THIS MESS.
IT'S ALL ON US NOW.

I, UH...
OWN SOME OF YOUR FILMS.
OH...
THANK YOU VERY MUCH.
TO BE HONEST... LOOKING AT YOU UP CLOSE ...
YOU'RE REALLY, UH.
PRETTY.
OH? YOU'RE SWEET.
WE'RE GOING TO PROTECT YOU WITH OUR LIVES.
YOU'LL BE OKAY.

HWOOOOOO

EPISODE 35: SOARING

EPISODE 35
バラバラ WHUP
バラバラ WHUP
バラバラ WHUP
バラバラ WHUP
バラバラ WHUP
THE PORN STAR?
ゴオオオオオオ
YOU DON'T KNOW?
IT'S PAPICO.
SHE SAVED ALL OUR ASSES.
WHAT'S SHE WEARING?
GEAR SENT IN FROM THE STATES.
THEY SAY IT'S SUPER-ELASTIC MATERIAL.
THE STATES? LIKE, NASA TECH?
WHY'S SHE GOT THAT ON?

ブォォ
オ。。オ。。オ。。
オ。。オ。。オ。。オ。。オ。。

MISSION'S EASY ENOUGH. ALL WE GOTTA DO...
IS MAKE SURE THAT CHICK OVER THERE GETS TO SHINJUKU.
ゴオオオオ
HWOOOOOOO
WHICH CHICK?

THIS'LL BE MY FIRST REAL ACTION.
IT'S THE SAME FOR ALL OF US.
WHAT'S GOING ON OUT THERE, ANY-WAY?
NO IDEA.
THEY HAVEN'T BRIEFED US YET.
LIKE... IS THERE REALLY ANYTHING OUT THERE?
WE'RE EN ROUTE NOW ...
SO OF COURSE THERE IS.
WE DON'T GOT A CHOICE.
WE GOTTA DO WHAT WE GOTTA DO.
RELAX, IT'S NOT LIKE THIS IS WAR.
WE'RE NOT UP AGAINST THE U.S. OR CHINA.

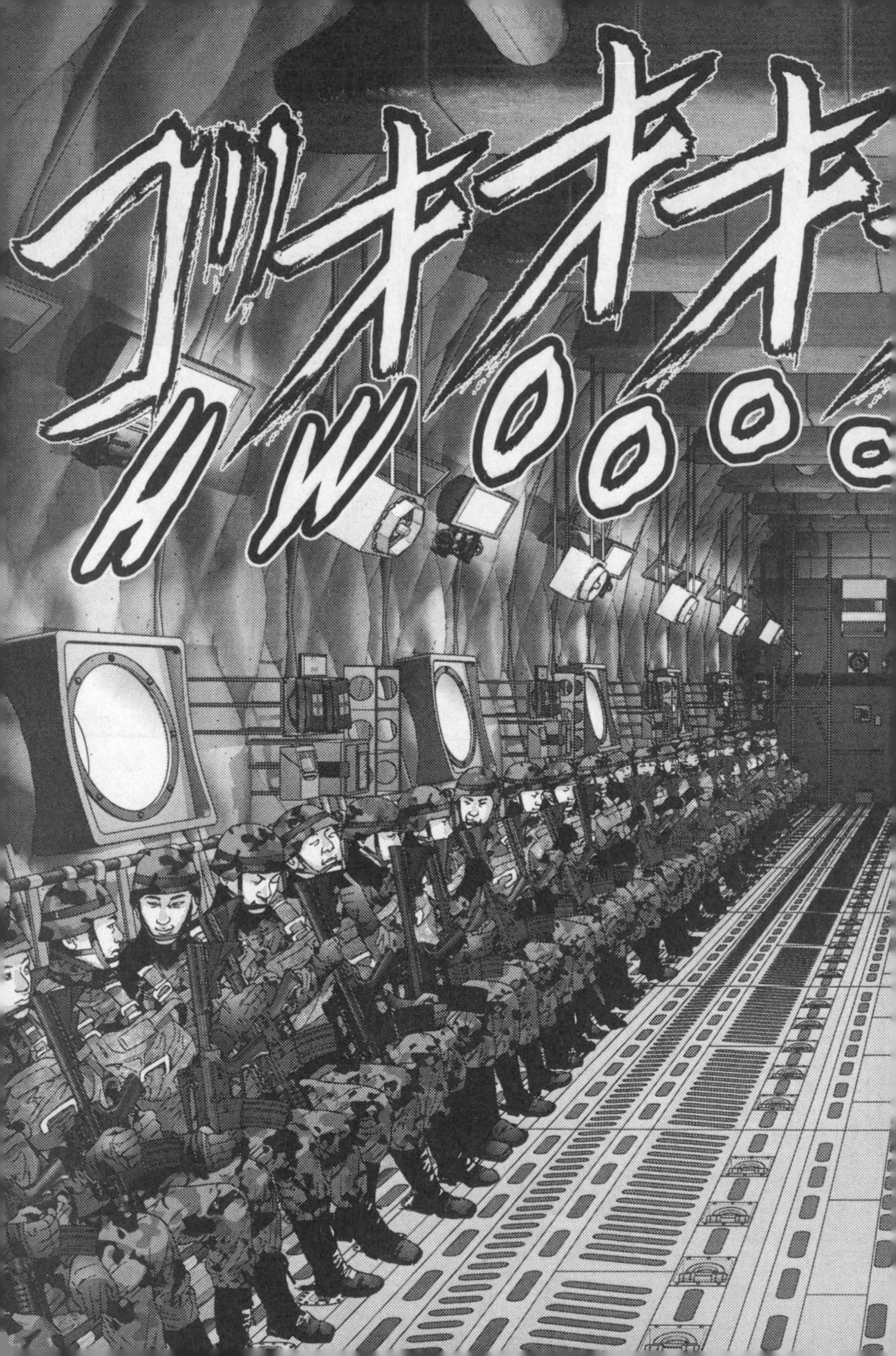

ゴオオオ
HWOOOO

オオオオ

バラ
WHUP
バ
WHUP

WHUP
WHUP
WHUP
WHUP

<This way! Come with me!!>

BOOM
THOOOOOOM
AH!
AAAH!
THOOM
THOOM
OH GOD... OH GOD...
THOOOOOOOM
BOOM

HUFF!
PANT!
PANT!
HUFF!
HUFF!
HUFF!
MPD
HUFF!

OH! OH! OH!!
BOOM
YOU CAN'T STOP ME!!
I'M INVINCI-BLE!!

BOOM
RAAAAH!

COME ON! JUST TRY IT!
BOOM
BOOM
BOOM
パチンコ
パスパス

HUFF!
HUFF!
HUFF!
HUFF!

WHAT'S WRONG? COME AT ME!
BOOM
QUIT FUCKING AROUND AND JUST KILL ME ALREADY !!
BOOM
BOOM
BOOM
HEEYYY!
BOOM

THOOOOOOM
HYAAAAAH!!
BOOM
BOOM

JUST TRY AND CRUSH ME!
DO IT, YOU BAS-TARDS!

BOOM
BOOM
BOOM
BOOM
カラオケの達人
BOOM
BOOM

MURMUR MURMUR MURMUR
EEEK!
SHWOOOO
BOOM
RUMBLE RUMBLE RUMBLE
RUMBLE RUMBLE RUMBLE RUMBLE
RUMBLE RUMBLE RUMBLE
IT'S NO USE.
IT'S... ALL OVER.

SHWOOOOO

EPISODE 34: OVER THERE

CLR
ENT
TW SYS

EPISODE 34
JOHANS-
SON.

BOOM
BOOM
BOOM
BOOM
BOOM

ドゴーン
BOOM

BOOOM

RRRR

RUMBLE
World elevator
Love your life.
「ラブエレ」
KUJITEC
クジテック株式会社
岡松セントラルビル
P
24H

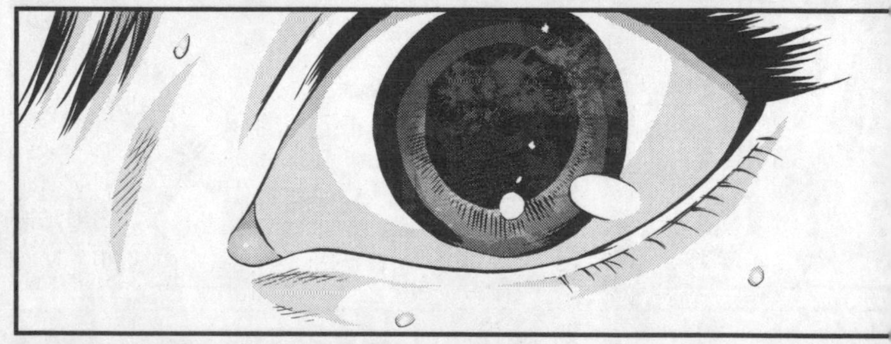

BOOM
BOOOM
BOOOM

World elevator.
Love your life.
[ラブエレ]
地球のエレベータ
KUJITEC
BOOM

AKAKARA
BOOM
BOOM

BOOM
BOOM
UWA-AAAH! WE'RE GONNA DIE!!
BOOM
EYYY-AAAH!

BOOM
BOOM

UHH-
HHN!
BOOM
BOOM
BOOM
BOOM
Let's
GO!

BOOM
MAAA-MAAA!
MA-MAAAA!

BOOM
BOOM
MPD
BOOM
BOOM

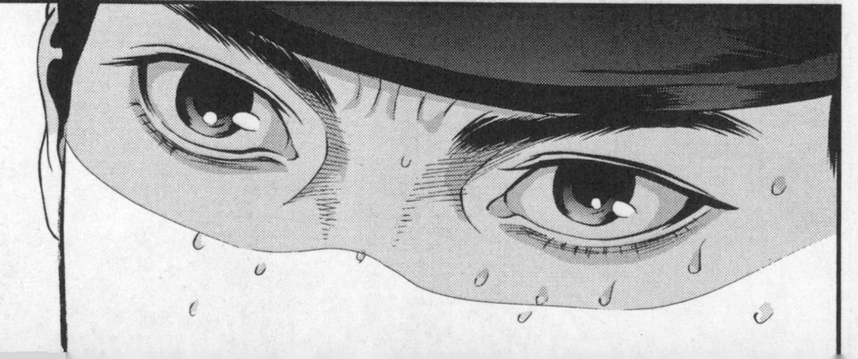

BOOM
<Nooooo!>
<Why?! Why, God?!>
AAAAAHHH!

BOOM
RURBERRY

S LUITT
OUIS LUITTO
BOOM
BOOM
BOOM

GYAAH!
KA-BOOM
GAH!!!

ぎゃあああああ
GYAAAAAAH!
KA-BOOM
HUFF!
HUFF!
KA-BOOM
KA-BOOM
HUFF!
HUFF!
KA-BOOM
KA-BOOM

HUFF!
BA-
DUMP
BA-
DUMP
HUFF!
HUFF!
HUFF!
BA-
DUMP
HUFF!
BA-
DUMP
BA-
DUMP
BA-
DUMP
BA-
DUMP
BA-
DUMP

# EPISODE 33: PUPIL

WAA-AAH! MAAA-MAAAA!
BOOM

BOOM
きゃあああ
EEEEEEK!

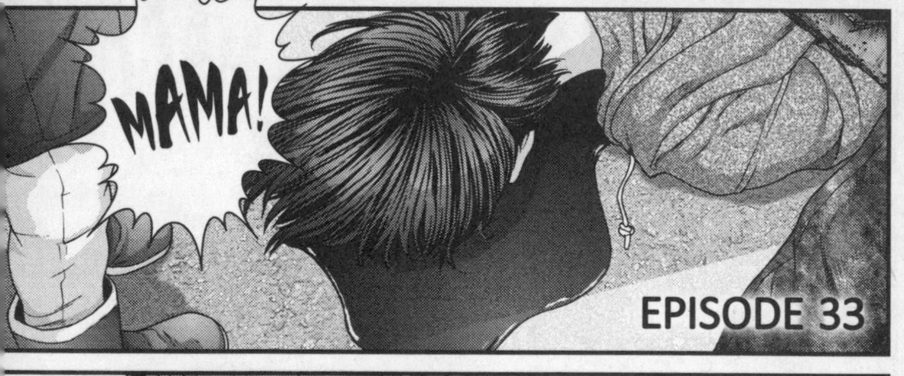
MAMA!
EPISODE 33

MAMA-AAA!
MAAAA-MAAAA!

BOOM
BOOM

B-Breath
Victory
Victory
Golf
Victory
JAR
Victory
B-Breath

MUOO-OOM!
MU-OOO-OM!
I DON'T WANT TO DIE!
I DON'T WANT TO DIE!!
BOOM

HUFF!
HUFF!
HUFF!
HUFF!
HUFF!
HUFF!
HUFF!
HUFF!
NO! NO!!
MOM! MOM!!
I DON'T WANT TO DIE!

BOOM
BOOM
BOOM
EEEK!
BOOM
BOOM
BOOM
OH, NO!
HUFF!
HUFF!
BOOM
HUFF!
NO!
BOOM

ドオーン
BOOM
ドーン
BOOM
ドーン
BOOM

BOOM

BOOOM
FWOOOOOOOO
WHUNCH

AAAAAAH!
AAAAGH!
BOOM
BOOM
BOOM
BOOM

THOOOOOM

CAN'T WE JUST HIDE HERE?!
WHOOM
WAA-AAA-AAH!
HUH?! WHAT THE?!
IT'S COM-ING BACK!!
THOOOOOOM

THOOM
OH GOD! OH GOD!
WE'RE ALL GONNA DIE!
THOOOOOM
MOM! MOM!!
PANT!
PANT!
PANT!
WAIT!
WHICH WAY DO WE GO?!
I DON'T KNOW!
THOOOOOM
THOOM

BOOM
LUMINE 2

THOOM
THOOOOM
THOOOOM
WHOA. WHAT IS THAT?
ARE YOU KIDDING ME?!
IT'S... THAT THING FROM E.T.E. AGAIN ...

WHOOOOM
WHOOOOM
THOOOOM
WHAT? NOW WHAT? WHAT'S HAPPENING?
AN EARTHQUAKE?!
ARE YOU KIDDING?
AN EARTHQUAKE?!
YOU SURE?
THOOOOM
WHAT IS THIS? WHAT'S GOING ON?

BOOM
BOO
BOOM

BOOM
EPISODE 32: DEBRIS

# EPISODE 32

LOOK AT SHINJUKU NOW!
BREAKING NEWS
MULTIPLE MONSTERS RAMPAGE

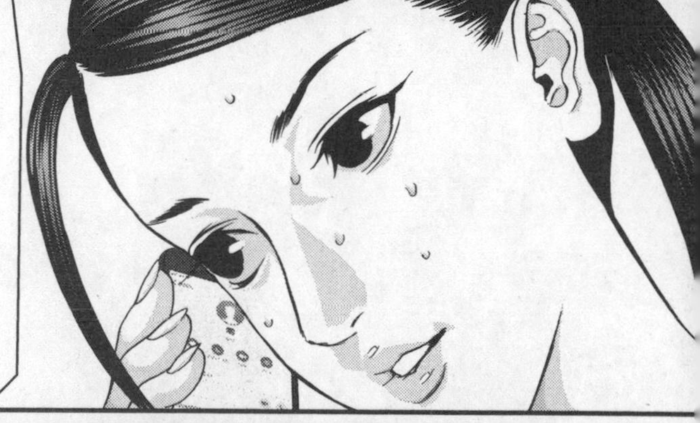
IS THERE ANY END TO THIS CRISIS?!

LOCAL
IS THIS HUMANITY'S MIDNIGHT HOUR? ARE THESE THE END TIMES?

オオオオオオオオ
HWOOOOOOO
東京都庁 →
東京都議会議事堂 →

パチンコ
パスパス
NO WAY!! NO WAY!!
I'M SCARED!! I'M SCARED!!
WHAT'S TAKING THE TRAIN?!
LET US OUT!!

ザワ
MURMUR
ザワ
MURMUR
ザワ
MURMUR

ザワ
MURMUR
ザワ
MURMUR
ワ
MURMUR
ザワ
MURMUR
ザワ
MURMUR

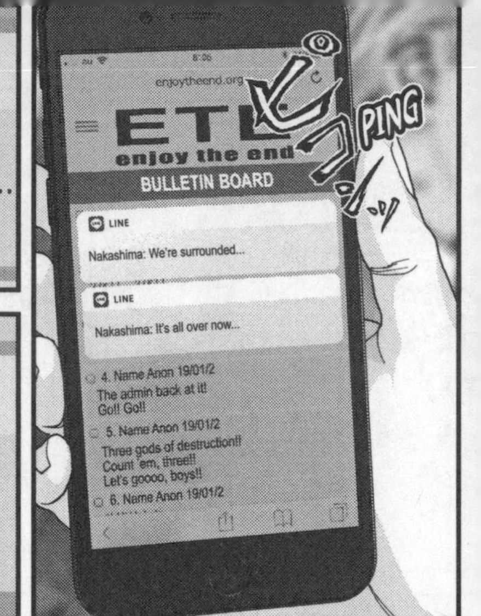

enjoytheend.org
ETL
enjoy the end
BULLETIN BOARD
LINE
Nakashima: We're surrounded...
LINE
Nakashima: It's all over now...
4. Name Anon 19/01/2
The admin back at it!
Go!! Go!!
5. Name Anon 19/01/2
Three gods of destruction!!
Count 'em, three!!
Let's goooo, boys!!
6. Name Anon 19/01/2
PING

LINE

Nakashima: We're surrounded...

LINE

Nakashima: It's all over now...

BULLETIN BOARD

1. Name Anon 19/01/16 (Wed) 09:43:21 No.

Go!! Go!!

2. Name Anon 19/01/21 (Mon) 08:02:14 No.

Three!! Three!!

3. Name Anon 19/01/21 (Mon) 08:02:15 No.

There's three of them!

5. Name Anon 19/01/2 (Mon)

Three gods of destruction!!
Count 'em, three!!
Let's goooo, boys!!

グラ RUMBLE
グラ RUMBLE
グラ RUMBLE
グラ RUMBLE

グラ RUMBLE
グラ RUMBLE
グラ RUMBLE
グラ RUMBLE
グラ RUMBLE
グラ RUMBLE
グラ RUMBLE
グラ RUMBLE

ザワ MURMUR
ザワ MURMUR
ザワ MURMUR
ザワ MURMUR
ザワ MURMUR
ザワ MURMUR
ザワ MURMUR
ザワ MURMUR
ザワ MURMUR
ザワ MURMUR

NOW MAKING AN EMERGENCY STOP...
SKKKRREEEEEEEE
RUMBLE
RUMBLE
RUMBLE

RUMBLE
RUMBLE
RUMBLE
RUMBLE
RUMBLE
RUMBLE
RUMBLE
RUMBLE
RUMBLE

HUH?
8:02
January 21 Monday
Early Warning
Early Warning
This is an earthquake early warning.
An earthquake has hit Tokyo Bay.
Please be ready for strong aftershocks.
(National Weather Service)
Swipe for more info

AH...

**PaPiCo**

@ PaPiCo0209 Follows you

I'm PaPiCo, Adult Actress.

Japan

Born September 17

Joined December 2011

588 Following 5568946 Followers

NO WAY ...

d December 2011

5568946 Followers

CHIHO-SAN... HAS 5.56 MILLION FOLLOW-ERS.
EVEN THOUGH SHE'S NO LONGER TWEET-ING.

ムンス
インターネット
コミックカフェ

アイアル
4F
小杉歯科医院
アイアル 4F
3F
入口
ハハマンショップ
猫の学校
2F
PFC
TOKYO STAY

4
57
137
Kuro Mia-san liked this
ELITA-1 @potp26 - 1h
Abe, how can you call that a military success?! 100,000 people have died, and he still won't pardon PaPiCo. Abe's a murderer.
4
6
Kogu-chan on hiatus @siege005
Hurry up and block ETE!
SWIPE
SWIPE
Black Manta @blackmant - 5m
Honestly, my opinion of the SDF has been turned around. Guess we didn't need PaPiCo after all?
Huntless @helenaway - 2m
Tasteful Gentleman @hon_masi
What's so fun about killing people in the Kanto area? I wish these country kids would fuck off already
1
2
2
Arthur @ King of the Sea

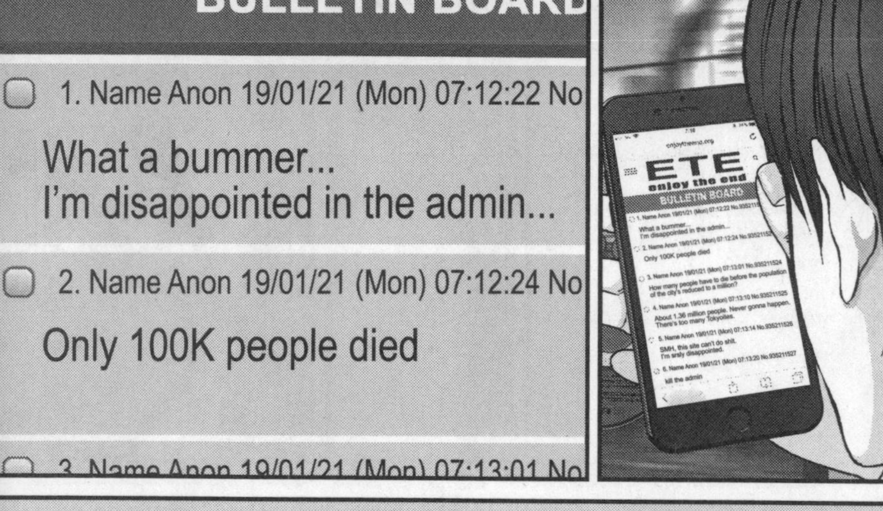
BULLETIN BOARD
1. Name Anon 19/01/21 (Mon) 07:12:22 No
What a bummer...
I'm disappointed in the admin...
2. Name Anon 19/01/21 (Mon) 07:12:24 No
Only 100K people died
ETE
enjoy the end
BULLETIN BOARD

3. Name Anon 19/01/21 (Mon) 07:13:01 No.935211524 del

How many people have to die before the population of the city's reduced to a million?

4. Name Anon 19/01/21 (Mon) 07:13:10 No.935211525 del

About 1.36 million people. Never gonna happen.
There's too many Tokyoites.

5. Name Anon 19/01/21 (Mon) 07:13:14 No.935211526 del

SMH, this site can't do shit.
I'm srsly disappointed.

6. Name Anon 19/01/21 (Mon) 07:13:20 No.935211527 del

ALL OF SHIBUYA FLATTENED: CASUALTIES EXCEED 100,000
CAN WE TRUST THE GOVERNMENT?
SPECIAL FEATURE: WHO IS PAPICO?
HER HISTORY, TRUE IDENTITY,
AND THE MYSTERY OF HER GIGANTISM
SIGNATURES DEMAND CHIHO
JOHANSSON'S RELEASE
渋谷壊滅…
死者・負傷者十万人超
政府発表は信用できるか？
パピコ履歴書
署名運動 急激増加
パピコを釈放せよ！
AREA
巨大ロボット撃破
自衛隊 快挙！
今、この世界で一体何が起こっているのか？
パピコの釈放
貴方は賛成？反対？
週刊文秋
安部首相
パピコは釈放せず
現政権の正念場
選挙に向けた判断？
国際的な批判も
GIANT ROBOT DEFEATED
IN MAJOR WIN FOR THE JSDF!
WHAT IS HAPPENING TO OUR WORLD RIGHT NOW?
MILITARY BUDGET INCREASE BECOMES MAJOR ELECTORAL TALKING POINT

100

自動

EPISODE 31: SURROUNDED CITY

REBEL
REBEL

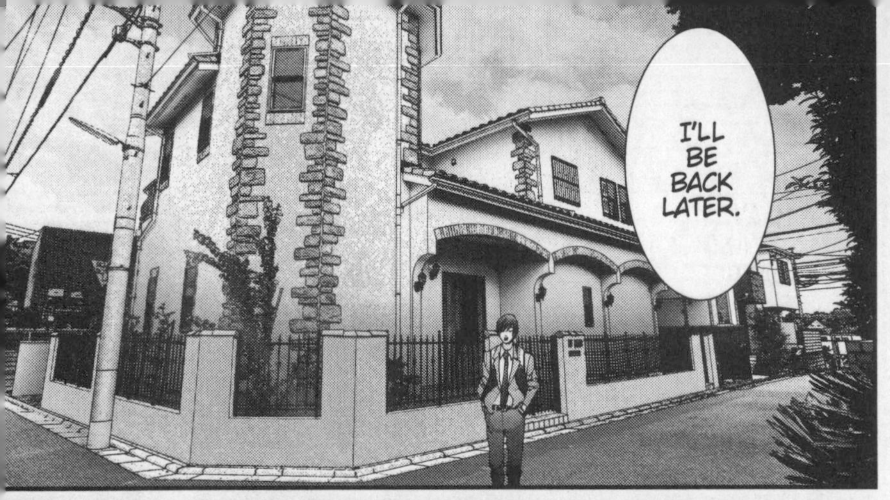
I'LL BE BACK LATER.

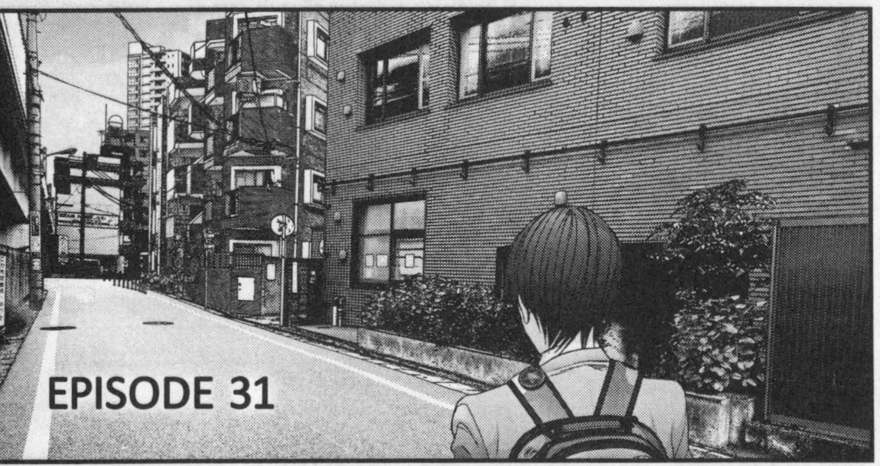

EPISODE 31

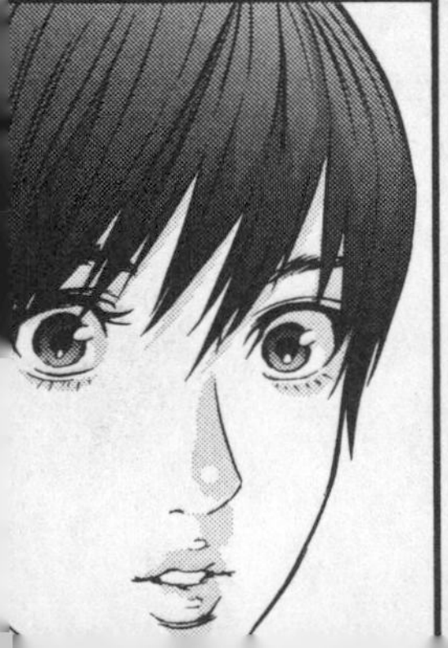

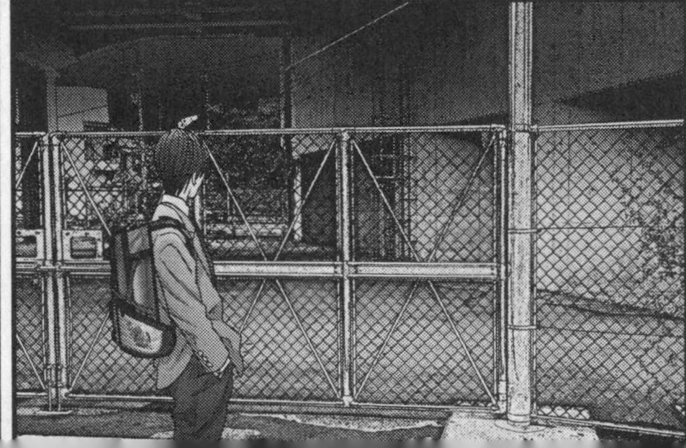

THE SELF-DEFENSE FORCES' MANEUVERS WERE A STUNNING SUCCESS.
HOWEVER, THEIR MILITARY STRENGTH SUFFERED A HEAVY BLOW, AND CASUALTIES ARE STILL BEING TALLIED.

Prime Minister
Live
Latest Cabinet Briefing
I WAS WRONG ABOUT THEM!
THOSE SDF GUYS ARE INCREDIBLE! AMAZING!!

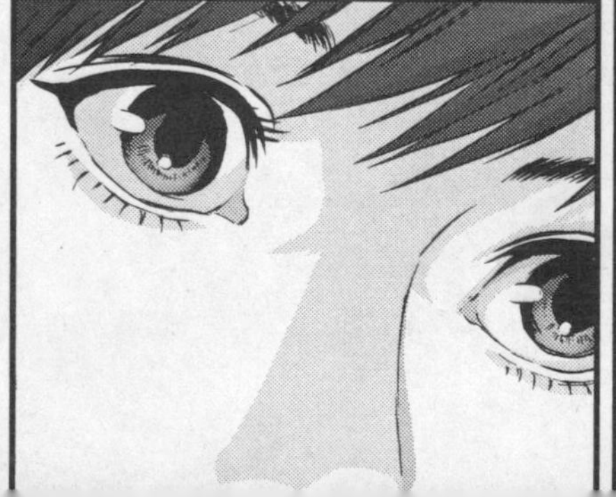

THOOM
THOOM

THOOM

BREAKING NEWS
SELF-DEFENSE FORCES ATTACK
AWWW, HELL YEAH!

BOOM
BOOM
BOOM

BOOM

YouTube
CALLING FOR PaPiCo'S RELEASE!
[PLEASE RT] CALLING ALL PAPICO SUPPORTERS: UNITE! RAISE YOUR VOICES FOR HER RELEASE!!!! [SUPPORT VIDEO]
2ND GENERATION JASON RED HOOD – 36 MILLION VIEWS – 1 DAY AGO
CALLING FOR PaPiCo'S RELEASE! EVERYONE SIGN THE PETITION!!

YEAH, PAPICO'S LIKE OUR LAST HOPE.
THE WHOLE COUNTRY AGREES.

ABE-SAN, ARE YOU AT HOME?
ARE YOU WATCHING TV?

OOO-OH!

OOO-OOH!

PEW
PEW
PEW
PEW
PEW
BA-BA-BOOM
BA-BOOM
CRUNCH

BOOM
BOOM
THE SELF-DEFENSE FORCES' JOINT EFFORTS APPEAR TO HAVE THE ROBOT OFF BALANCE!!
AAAH! THE ASSAULT'S WORKING!!

BOOM
BOOM
BOOM
BOOM
BOOM
パチンコ

SHIBUYA HAS BECOME A SEA OF FLAMES!
THE GIANT ROBOT LAYS WASTE TO THE CITY AS IT MAKES ITS WAY TOWARD SHINJUKU!

# enjoy the end

## BULLETIN BOARD

1. Name Anon 19/01/16 (Wed) 09:43:21 No. 734211512 del +

That's what you geeeet!
That's what you get, Tonkin town!

2. Name Anon 19/01/16 (Wed) 09:43:24 No. 734211523 del +

Shibuya is toooaaast!

ガガ
RUUUUMMMBLE
ッ

バラ WHUP
バラ WHUP
バラ WHUP
バラ WHUP
バラ WHUP

バラ WHUP
バラ WHUP
バラ WHUP
バラ WHUP
バラ WHUP

 6800

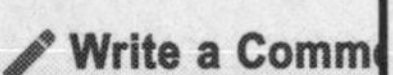
Write a Comm

Rodimus*** | 1 Hour Ago

**I told you!!**
Let PaPiCo out already.
So many lives lost.
When will you wake up?!

84 Replies

55950

HAAAH.
ARE WE... GOING TO BE OKAY...?

Anonymous | 1 Hour Ago

Our own government has Japanese blood on their hands! They're murdering people every minute PaPiCo's locked up. Free PaPiCo. They should bow down before her and let her end this!

Free PaPiCo, you assholes!

Free PaPiCo!

**Prime Minister Abe declares current events impossible to link conclusively to E.T.E. JSDF to spare no effort fighting the threat.**

1/16 (Sat) 8:50 a.m.

Daily Bugle
DB.com

 **7369**

SHIBUYA! OH, GOD! SHIBUYA HAS BECOME A SCENE STRAIGHT OUT OF HELL!!
WHUMP
COMMERCIAL BREAK? ALL RIGHT, WE'RE CUTTING TO COMMERCIAL.

N-NOW FOR A STATEMENT FROM PRIME MINISTER ABE.
BREAKING NEWS

AAAAGH! FACED WITH AN UNBEAT-ABLE FOE...
THE SELF-DEFENSE FORCES ARE RETREAT-ING!
LIVE
THE SELF-DEFENSE FORCES ARE-- AAAGH!
THEY'RE RUNNING AWAY!! AAAAH!!
WHUP バラ
WHUP バラ
WHUP バラ
IS THIS... IS THIS REALLY HAPPENING?! ARE THINGS REALLY SO HOPELESS?!
JA44HH
WHUP バラ
WHUP バラ

BOOM

BOOM
BOOM
BOOM
BOOM
BOOM

BOOM
BOOM

KA-
BOOM
AND
Hyecity
フルスキン
クリニック
コンタクトの
ハイシティ

BSSHT
THOOM
BSSHT
THOOM

THOOM
バラ
WHUP
バラ
WHUP
バラ
WHUP
バラ
WHUP
EPISODE 30: ROBOT
D·light

バラ
WHUP
バラ
WHUP
バラ
WHUP
バラ
WHUP
ズシン
THOOM
ANH
JA97NH
SEIBU

# EPISODE 30

WHAT IS THIS?! THIS IS STRANGER THAN FICTION. IT'S LIKE AN ANIME OR HOLLYWOOD FILM!
BUT THIS...! A REAL GIANT ROBOT IN SHIBUYA!!
BREAKING NEWS
GIANT ROBOT APPEARS IN SHIBUYA!!
Live
EPISODE 30

WHAT... IS... GOING... ON...?

......

NO... NO, NO, NO.
NOT GOOD.

WHAT... IS... THAT?
ズ THA-
ズ THOOM
ン

THE SELF-DEFENSE FORCES ARE RETREAT-ING.
THERE'S NOTHING THEY CAN DO AGAINST THIS THING!!
THOOM
ズ
ン
ズ
ズ
THA-
THOOM
ン

アイアル
アロム

THOOM
天皇賞(冬)
1月28日
LETTERS

DSH DSH DSH DSH
RAT-A-TAT-A-TATAT
WOW, THIS IS CRAZY ...
RAT-A-TATAT
RAT-A-TATAT

SHOULD THEY BE SHOWING THIS ON TV?

I THINK I'LL HOP OUT TO THE STORE REALLY QUICK.

1. Name Anon 19/01/16 (Wed) 07:52:20

Robot!! Robot!!
Robot!! Robot!!

2. Name Anon 19/01/16 (Wed) 07:52:24

Giant Robot!!
Giant Robot!!

3. Name Anon 19/01/16 (Wed) 07:52:28

Robot!! Robot!!
Robot!!

2. Name Anon

Giant Robot!!
Giant Robot!!

3. Name Anon 19/01/1

Robot!! Robot!!
Robot!!

AAAH! FOLKS, LOOK AT THIS!!

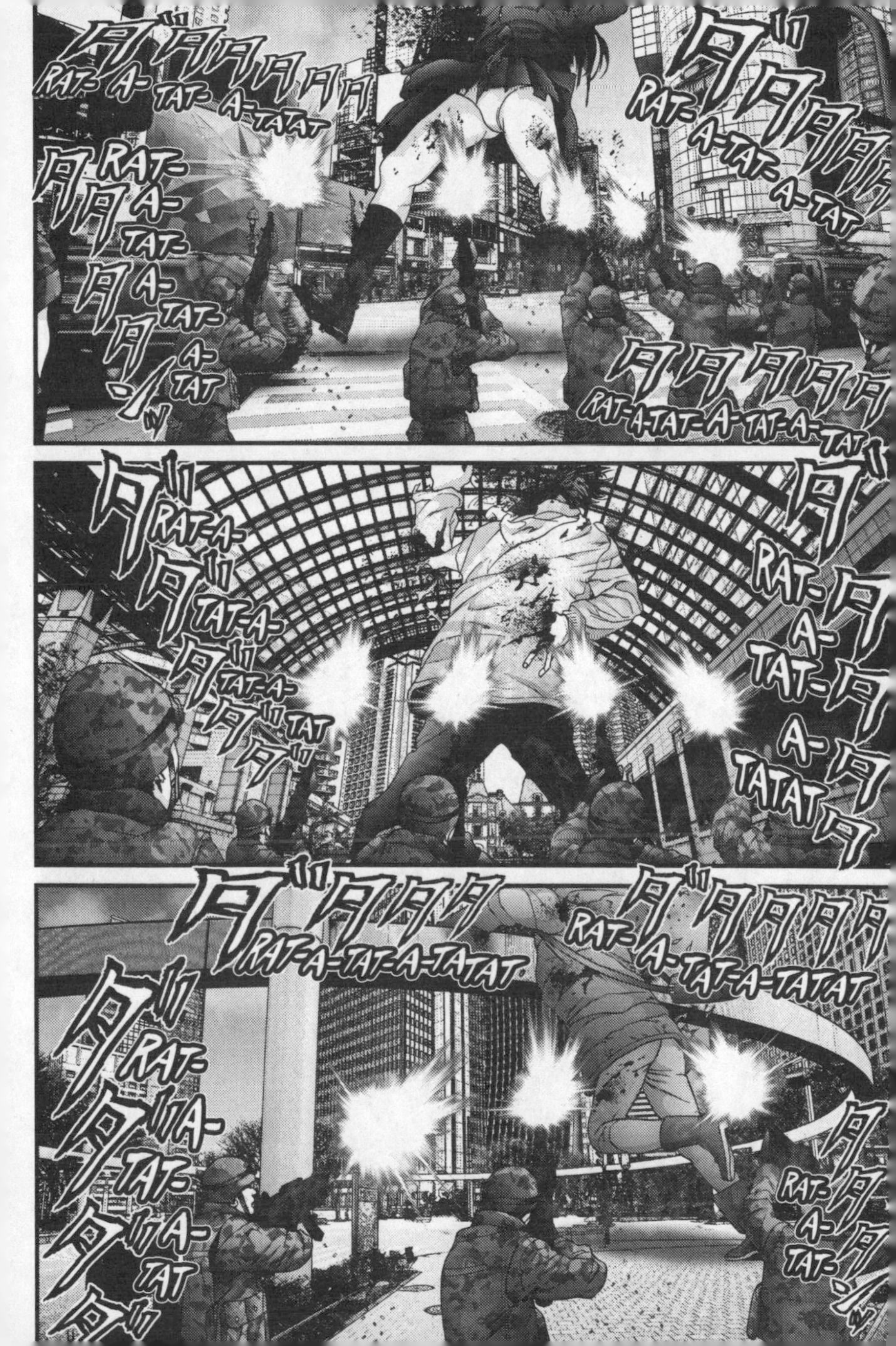
RAT-A-TAT-A-TAT
RAT-A-TAT-A-TATAT
RAT-A-TAT-A-TAT-A-TAT
RAT-A-TAT-A-TAT-A-TAT
RAT-A-TAT-A-TATAT
RAT-A-TAT-A-TAT-A-TAT
RAT-A-TAT-A-TATAT
RAT-A-TAT-A-TATAT
RAT-A-TAT-
RAT-A-TAT-A-TAT

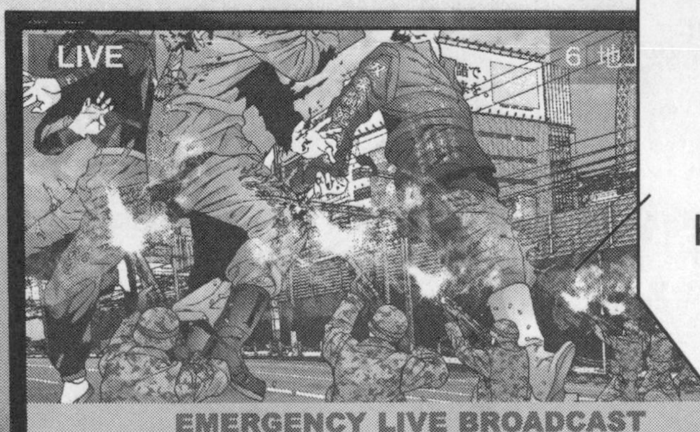
LIVE
6
EMERGENCY LIVE BROADCAST
SELF-DEFENSE FORCES BEGIN ASSAULT ON GIANT UNIDENTIFIED CREATURES OF UNKNOWN ORIGIN INVADING TOKYO.
THE SELF-DEFENSE FORCES HAVE JUST OPENED FIRE!!

RAT-A-TAT-A-TAT
RAT-A-TAT-A-TAT
RAT-A-TAT-A-TAT
RAT-A-TAT
RAT-A-TAT-A-TAT-A-TAT

**Committee for the Release of PaPiCo** @savethe...- 10h
[Pls RT] We demand PaPiCo-san's immediate release!!

PaPiCo-san stopped the Roppongi giant in 2hrs. She's our only hope against Tokyo's rampaging giants!

The surveillance footage submitted as evidence to District Court 1 failed to prove PaPiCo-san crushed or injured any civilians.

The Tokyo district court won't acknowledge that fact. Toss her sentence now!

**[Pls RT]** We demand PaPiCo-san's immediate release!!

PaPiCo is innocent.

Release our real hero!!

Serves you rmignt

2. Name Anon 19/01/16 (Wed) 07:08:59 No.611115

You can do it! We're so close to Tokyo b
Just keep it up!!

3. Name Anon 19/01/16 (Wed) 07:09:07 No.611115

Guys... If the city of Tokyo's infrastructu
down...it'll affect us in the countryside, t

4. Name Anon 19/01/16 (Wed) 07:09:22 No.611115

Tokyo's full of nothing but scumbags, so
can die for all I care.

I CAN'T BELIEVE THESE GUYS.

Kaiteuyusa @eveparadise - 30s
At 2 a.m. this morning, I lost my mother
#unconfirmedcatastrophe
Six Flowers @shatteredmega - 50s
I couldn't sleep at all.
This is too scary...
Yuuta @cliffjump - 57s
My neighborhood this morning

AH... SCHOOL.
IT'S BEEN CANCELED.


1-F Communicatio

There's no school too
Everyone please stay
home and be safe.

As soon as we see h
this all goes down, w
contact you again.

I HOPE THEY CAN CLEAR THIS MESS UP BY THE END OF TODAY.

SERI-OUSLY. I CAN'T GO SHOP-PING LIKE THIS.

ETE
enjoy the en

Bulletin Board

1. Name Anon 19/01/16 (Wed) 07:08:52 No.61111522

Serves you right, Tokyo.
Serves you riiiiight

2. Name Anon 19/01/16 (Wed) 07:08:59 No.61111523

HERE WE CAN SEE THE SELF-DEFENSE FORCES CONVOY.
THEY'VE BEEN ROLLING INTO THE CITY SINCE DAWN.

WEE-OO WEE-OO
WEE-OO WEE-OO WEE-OO
WEE-OO WEE-OO
BWOOP BWOOP BWOOP BWOOP BWOOP

BWOOP BWOOP BWOOP BWOOP
BZZT BZZT BZZT BZZT

SON OF A BITCH!
DAMN YOU ALL TO HELL!

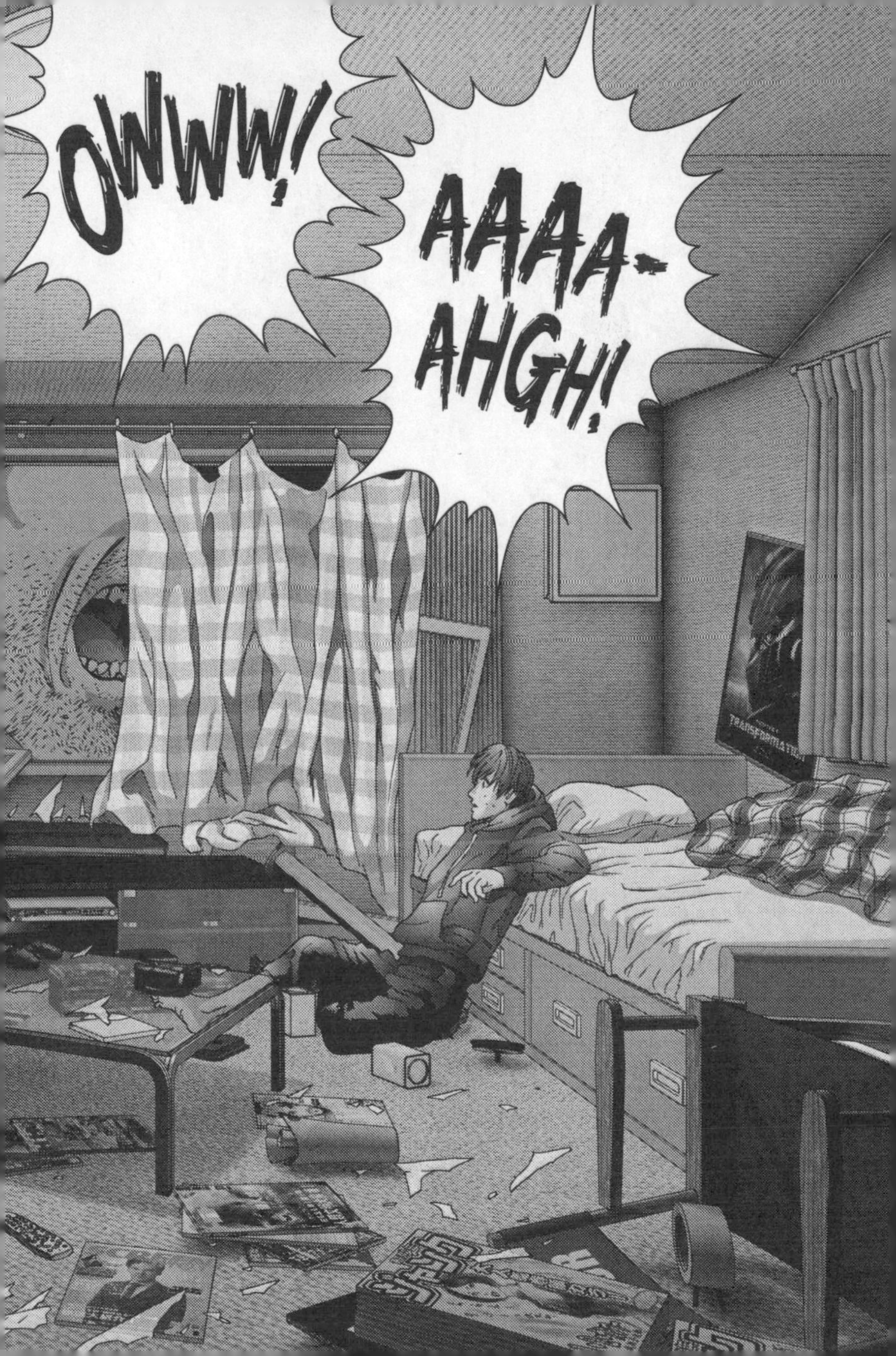
AAAA-AHGH!
OWWW!

SHRRRAK
キ!!キ!!キ!!
AA-AUGH! THAT HURT!

REI!!
THIS WAY!!
REI!!

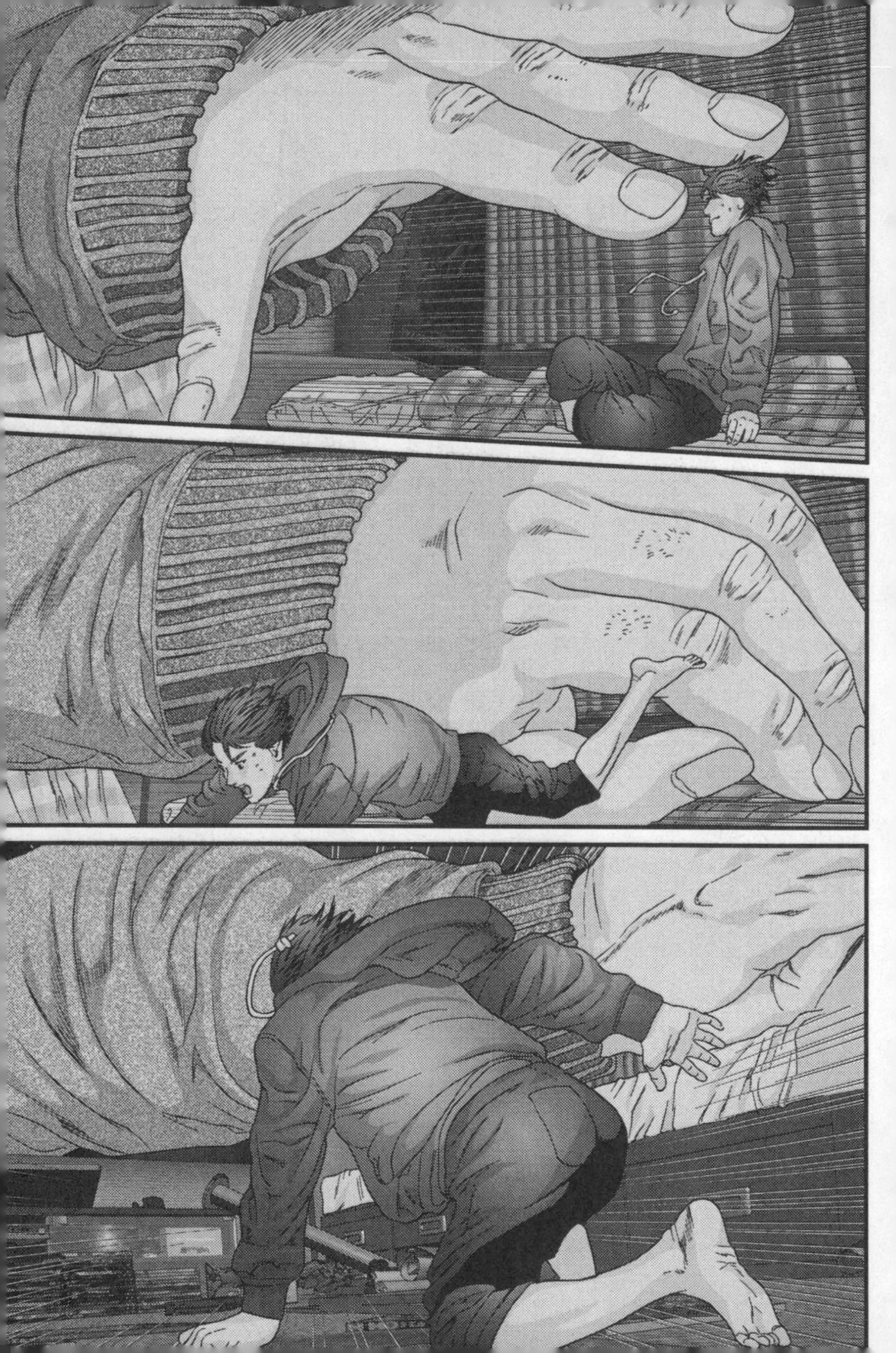

REI!
REI!!
ARE YOU ALL RIGHT ?!

REI !!

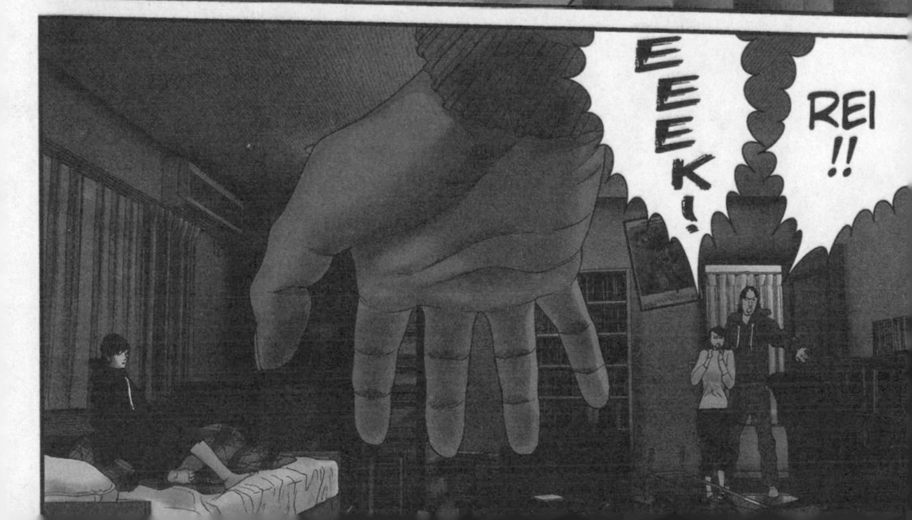
REI !!
EEEEK!!

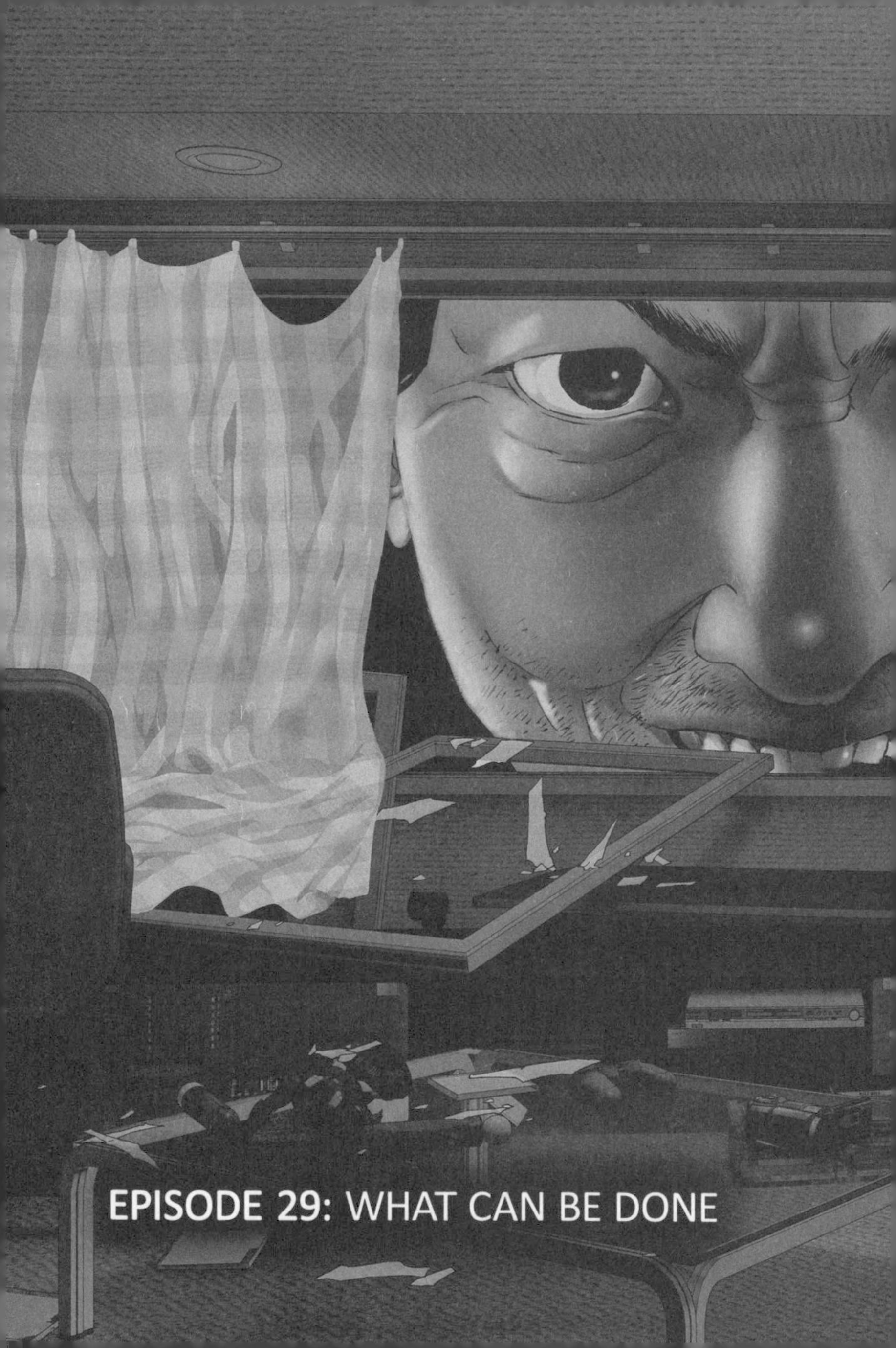
EPISODE 29: WHAT CAN BE DONE

GOT ONE.

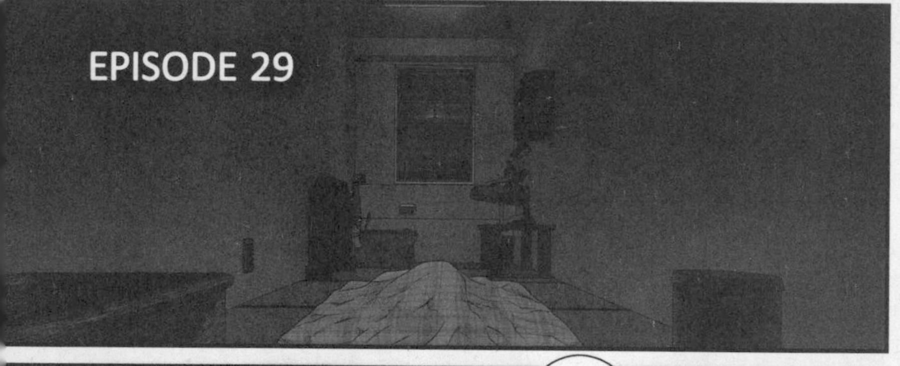
EPISODE 29

REI... KUN...